WHOOP & SHUSH

WHOOP & SHUSH

poems Jeff Baker

LOST HORSE PRESS
Sandpoint, Idaho

Cover Art by April Joy Baker. "Two Foxes," 6.5" x 7.5" redbud leaves / hornets' nest.
Author Photo: April Joy Baker.
Book & Cover Design by Christine Holbert.

This and other fine LOST HORSE PRESS titles may be viewed online at www.losthorsepress. org.

FIRST EDITION

LIBRARY OF CONGRESS CATALOGING-IN-PUBLICATION DATA

Baker, Jeff, 1972-
[Poems. Selections]
Whoop & shush : poems / by Jeff Baker.—First edition.
     pages cm ISBN 978-0-9908193-0-1 (alk. paper)
I. Title. II. Title: Whoop and shush.
PS3602.A58646A6 2015
811'.6—dc23
                                        2014044439

CONTENTS

for Charlotte, April, and Amelia Rose

I

LOUIS vs. LOUIS

Call me Louis. There is my great enemy,
Louis! Louis hops around the junkyard,
stovepipes on his legs to protect himself
from vipers. Louis reads in the dark his
clarinet. Louis walks downtown wearing
a look that says, *I am a terrible man.*
Dare not entreat to speak to me now
or ever. I believe our connection was
leaky somewhere, in the phone lines
or the floorboards. When we met, Louis
offered to shine my shoes. I said, *No.*
Louis offered to cut me with his boot
razor. I said, *Louis, shine my shoes!*
Bless the tides of slaughter that brought
this Louis to my side, the regrettable
but necessary murders and immolations,
the blood histories it took to produce
Louis the pulsing tooth—Louis
the mournful harmonica. Early winter,
leaves no longer hid the General's
warhorse on the square. I was ready
to offer Louis some of the monies
I'd earned for stacking bolts of fabric
next to the machines, but Louis had
withdrawn. I sought him everywhere:
in the bleared windows of each café,
in the early soup of commuters, beyond
the turnstiles and under the harbor
bridge. Then some nights I'd smell him
upwind of the bagel bakery, or I'd hear

his sublime cornet struck up upon
the waters. But I was lost. If my head
hadn't been wired on, I would've had
no yelp to go by. Louis the encounter—
Louis the complete darkness. I sit by
the river. Girls in a scull like a waterbug
shiver, with their oars, gray currents.
The man in his motorboat barks into
his bullhorn and steers. Waves slap.
The surface will hardly hold up a face.
Louis the bright symptom—Louis
the martyred stone. After the snakebite
it was Louis who took off my foot
at the ankle. He was what saved me.

GRACELAND

Guess I've found a new place to dwell.
　　　　All day I fire my .38
at a television the size of God. Being risen,
　　　　my kung fu jumpsuit
is so brilliant even the angels must look
　　　　away. And Christ is seen,
at a distance, fingering his ancient rags.

　　　　　　　　•

This ought to be the swingingest eternity
　　　　ever. But some nights
one improper shimmy of the hips turns
　　　　the jungle room to desert.
And all the Harem Scarem girls? Salt.
　　　　Then, centuries of sleep,
teeth floating around the head like thorns.

　　　　　　　　•

These sideburns descend all the way to Hell.
　　　　This happened long ago
when Lucifer cried Rapunzel and climbed
　　　　from the pit with his entourage:
minor demons wailing rockabilly, débutantes
　　　　in their burnt corsages,
then the sausage grinder (and his monkey).

•

I am not a product of the Elvis Presley Estate,
        but my heart still sings in
its colonnades of fat, the bones in my hands
        are still packed with suns.
Still, there are long nights when my face
        slides off like a cape, when
the wind leaving my body sighs *Graceland*.

•

The King don't leave a clambake 'til it's done.
        The girls all like to get
recumbent under my swaying grass skirts
        while I play both ukuleles
at once. The first I strum just to make the stars
        burn, while the other calls
out to the sea, saying: *c'mon, shake your ass.*

CALIBAN AT BIKINI

> "Be not afeared; the isle is full of noises,"
>
> —*The Tempest*

Prime Forger, long your cormorant wing
      has spanned me with its shadow.
Why is it I find me now anonce such strange-
      light? How paled by you
are the cuspate stars, the low sun poached
      in sea-mist. I crouch
to counterfeit a stone for fear your wish is
      to pilfer me, my dull carapace,
of its ever-abiding mum. But what use?
      I feel your marrow-gulls
plunging me to get swiftly at the matter,
      your impostor eyes trained
for some obscure wiggle in the receding
      foam. Rather to eat pumice
and vomit and tear out my throat, than to be
      plucked—to be halved
and halved like a fruit or some vague rumor
      of myself. Slyboots, fear me
not. So inscrutable is your guising, so mischief-
      proof your high alphabet, you
strike me dumb though your voice's graphs
      be blacked beneath my skin—
it is your device, whatever tooth of wit might
      swim my brain, so gnashing you
it is I alone I gnash. If you'll not now disown
      this luminance which ferrets me,

in fairness, give me the underearth for private
　　　　stealth, where I or some half-
doubling may rest, while your blinding hand
　　　　enumerates and resolves.

AFTER POWER IS RESTORED
AT THE MEAT PROCESSING PLANT

Hooked steel
tongs—a pair—
beneath red ice
in the zero room.

Who joined us
so? You and I
fulcrumed—we
cannot touch.

STORY

Near dusk we shot a buck. Twice we found
places where he'd fallen and rolled, fought
to get up as the foreign sound of our boots
came crisp through cold air. In those spots
the blood was black on the snow and it stank
like the undersides of moss. The trail
banked us down to a field of winter briars
where we lost the tracks and began to hunt
in widening circles for blood. There were
blood-trails on the undersides of clouds—
away from which the earth visibly rolled—
and I felt then my own stink, in me, welling
up. Circles moving out from the epicenter
of a dead animal hardening in snow—
other circles which close violently inward.

·

We couldn't tell the branches
from the briars—crouching

above the gully—the dog
he'd shot bawled in the thicket—

the wind had a body we could hear—
shaving down the ridgeline

toward us—nothing arrived—
third time out she wouldn't hunt—

explosion of blood at the haunches—
still she ran—home was far—

I was the smallest—he gave me
the .38—the sky ticked—

I pushed in—held the briars
to balance myself in the mud—

what she was saying in there—
untranslatable—do something

like that, you'll want to get close—
let out a half-breath—

plant your feet—
plant your body—

·

Once the whole family gathered in the yard
and we shielded our eyes against the sun
to watch a hawk circle lower and lower—
or, we watched the hawk's shadow move
slowly over the fields by our house while
my father wasted fourteen rounds attempting
the impossible shot. I watched as he levered
the last cartridge into the carbine's chamber.

I'm flying too close to the earth.

•

Running near dawn, my heart warbles.
My kneecaps are magnesium crucibles.

If I fall, two boys will find me and kick
my skull down railroad tracks toward

a shack where the skeleton of a hawk
is nailed to the door, where my father

steps out with a mailbag and a lantern,
where he takes me in and rests me upon

a pressboard table, where no one writes
there are other earths and skies than these

next to the candle which gives its light
to the creep of wax from which it burns.

CAMINANDO

"Sucede que me canso de ser hombre."

—*Walking Around*

Tired of being misbeing's dumb ancestors,
      Pablo and I walk around sad.
We idle in the gray season's intestinal light,
      backscatter sky where dingy
clouds collywobble. We mope past butchers'
      counters where round-faced
scales hang like bodiless owls—past bakers'
      cases where white smirks
of icing adorn the strudels' straitjackets.
      Pablo's bored by my beta waves
as astonishing as nits in an unkempt kid's
      cropped bangs. He's fed up
with my face like a hen roosting, with feigned
      attentiveness, over our attrition.
Pablo is weary even of our tails—extremities
      whipping in our vestigial wake.

Pablo sings his weariness the way a lion opens
      carotid caves that let slip the soul.
I sing along the way hind hooves leave a drag-
      trail pointing to the garish semiotic
of the carcass. We skulk past soupbone crowds
      of consumers. We skirt cafés where
the wine has legs—the liquid tentacles of wealth
      radiating down the rounded insides
of glasses. We side-step on duck-stuffed river

walks where the water squelches
into oubliettes beneath our feet and grumbles
        hydraulic, as of dysenteric viscera,
start up beyond the sewer's welded grates. We
        stoop in vestibules where umbrellas
hang. Pablo sings his weariness the way an orca
        tosses seal pups in the surf. I sing
the way rent flippers tidemark obsidian shores.

How weary I am of Pablo's hanging jowls—
        rinds of meat cured in the locker
where Joy grew moldy. I despise the sea-sweat
        odor of his little brown hat,
which reminds me of the rag nest the cur's
        pups keep to in their stump
of alleyway. I loathe Pablo's pants, white
        and skittery like the ghost-fur
of lab rats. I hate his cane, his gait fractured
        with age, the swells of his paunch,
his thudding, charcoal-colored orthopedics
        heavy as stones used to weight
heretics. I am weary of his eyes, murderous
        and angelic, which drown me
and baptize me at every glance. I can't fathom
        his lips rude red as the lily's
center where the stamen lifts its sex—beautiful
        animal lips which part and sing
the way raptors' talons lift salmon gasping
        toward ravenous nests. I sing
the way the sewer's piping rumbles toward
        its outlet hidden in cattails
by the microbial river. I sing the filthy murk

where even sun can't fix its nails
to flanks of gold-scaled carp as they hunker
and roll in timeless deep to feed.

JACKSONVILLE

I am creating an interior in miniature.

Imagine the likelihood — roots, cracked
      porcelain, musket balls, stone knockers,
and there in the earth my ragged ancestor —
      teeth and coffin nails in his acidic clay.

Our Sunday Kiss was a bedpan filled with wasps,
      stung slivers of starling-shriek,
convergent gases above the parking lot filling
      into your eyes the warmest greens.

There alligators, so white and fragile, were segregated
      and kept from sun. Vast systems
of sprinklers diluted the corporeal rain. At 6 pm
      the cannon will be fired upon the town.

Our Sunday Kiss was the dark, foreboding forest
      cut and stacked on truck beds.
Hung in the sky a single cloud — humped, immobile.
      Buffalo Ghost, sing me up there!

I'm eight! I'm really eight? barebacking the mule
      down out of the wrong century
with another log to unchain, length and load.
      Vultures of the gift shop, mock war clubs,

and soon the state pie wobbling forward, the sea
      a torched blue cellophane rolling

right up to the advertisements, someone arguing
    "old slave market" is merely a euphemism.

Our Sunday Kiss was a brick silo crumbling
        near the Castillo Reál, a dusk formed
wholly out of gunpowder, a briefer convoy
        in the long commute of the damned.

At the cockfight, the feathers of a grey cock flared
        like a Corona of Golden Knives.
Some still rattled in the deathheap behind the stands—
        we fed them mush and nursed them back.

In the painting of Golgotha the face of Christ—
        smaller, and more dimly lit,
than the skulls that lie around the cross. The nails
        are arrowpoints vectoring earthward.

Thinking, then oblivion. One is reminded
        swarming angels held raw night
to their wounds, while someone stood by
        their mailbox for hours . . .

Our Sunday Kiss is pouring its boxcars into the trees.

THREE FLUID GRACES

Moon is wearing
someone's polished skull
like a pith helmet.

This is when
we come to change
the pan of tears—

when we pull
body after body
from the reservoir.

Here is your
tongue, your claws,
steam which knocks

the pipes in
your chest. Here
are the wires to lace

your sternum shut,
cables for the pulleys
in your shoulder blades—

power lines
where your legs dead-
end at the crotch.

There will still be time
for a quick nap
at the gurney factory.

Dumb creature, we
kneel and wash you
with spit.

APRIL BLIZZARD

White whips of spindrift beneath the street lights'
                                        fission—
a snowdrift climbs the door one dare not open
                            like a cresting
wave—
            and though the softened light inside their hulls
suggests a giddy warmth,
                            the buses sign OUT OF SERVICE
and quit their routes.
                    The blocky ghost of a mailbox haunts
the corner where steam rises
                        from the bent mouth of a manhole.
Branches, bowed, soon begin
                        to break—then novas of downed
power lines—the mind in the dark contracting
                                        itself
like a dying star—densethought—
                            the body bending
its osseous ideogram towards sleep.
                        When it's like this, we
dally too sweetly with our lead shadows.
                        When it's like this,
the postmen come
                    approaching our darkened windows.
Is it difficult to believe green shoots
                        have pushed up beneath
the banks of snow and that, like so,
                        our dreads and joys record
themselves upon a single ground?

                              Postcard and postcard
and postcard fills up these idling
                              trucks parked side by side.
Tomorrow a blue suitcase, hidden
                              beneath the junipers,
will throw itself open.
                    Tomorrow birdsong, the reappearance
of a child's wagon
                    covered by snowplows, nature loosening
itself like a muscle that can kill.
                         Tomorrow a warm breeze
across a windowsill littered with capsized flies.
                                        Tomorrow
robins hopping
              their shabby goddamn scansion in the grass.

OUROBOROS

Before we wake, tell me again the one
        about how you died,
about how blood clotted your throat
        shut—before we wake
dream us back—writhe of watersnakes
        we found balled above
the flood—the hornets' nest in flame,
        you stoop and I pinch
the venom sack to pluck a stinger from
        your eye—show me
just where your skull caved—
        I'll show you how a living arm
extends from a dead man's shirt—

•

Bathwater kettled from the woodstove—
        dropped to my bath
(from the hole you left after the pipes froze)
        the rat—blind without
glasses I lower in and she bites—I catch
        her neck and hold her
until she drowns—behind the sheet rock
        her raw litter pulsing—

My shred shirt crimsons in the crown
        of a tulipifera you
close to killed me with—the saw idling
        for a moment while
you gauge from uphill my injuries—
        the loop of steel teeth—
blue fume of oil the engine exhales—

•

Ten squirrels twined to a swing set—
        my arms bloodless
by the time I yank the last hide free—
        tell me something
in dust-mouth before day's ingot
        comes to dress us
in its wound, before the sky is radiation
        and there's too much
earth—I'll tell you *I love you so much*—
        I'll strike a fire in
your whiskers with my fists—tell me
        there's nothing to drink
and I'm going to lean on you, press
        my muzzle in deep—

·

The hawk ratcheting down zero
        in the sky—the hens
voicing the same high, drawn-out croak—
        a chorus which means
in their language: *death descends*—

·

A fly sharpens its legs on an eyelash—
        the snake that no longer
exists is swallowing the snake that does—
        night and day—we
were together like a mouth stitched—
        unsuture the blue-
black and what will extend itself?

·

Hot my father's final breath rose
        into the room and one
standing over him stooped to push
        his jaw shut—tell me
again about the trout given back
        to the stream—how
the gills worked to fan red smoke
        into the water—

THE MECHANIC'S DAUGHTER

cleans her gamecock's feet and tarsi
      with alcohol on a swab.
She wraps the heels in gauze and slips
      over bony spurs, sawed
down to stubs, steel gaffs' leather cuffs
      and she fastens them
with waxed twine. Rooster weighed—
      5 lbs 8 oz—she traps
him under an arm to keep spangled
      wings from working
and draws over the curved shanks a fold
      of fine sandpaper.
Once I heard her sing at Citico Creek
      where she waded out
to be baptized—*Like a Virgin* instead
      of *Amazing Grace.*
Three burly deacons submerged her
      large and buoyant body
and when she rose a tobacco stain
      spread down her good
white shirt—snuff in a handkerchief
      stuffed amid her breasts.
The mechanic's daughter pits her rooster
      on the chalk. Wine dark
hackles flare around the vicious head.
      Weeks ago the blood-filled
comb was cut away and the raw crown
      capped with salve. She fed
him corn, egg and raw beef—trimmed
      away the flying feathers.

She lets him go and the fight is done.
　　　　He leaps and lands, gaffs
buried in the crop of another cock.
　　　　One Easter, at the mall,
three plastic torsos hung from slender
　　　　wires behind the glass.
How beautiful, she said. Nothing there
　　　　she could wear. At sunrise
service the pastor had warned how souls
　　　　flail in a river of fire.
She guessed her father must moan there.
　　　　Drunk, a blow torch
exploded in his face. He ran until he fell.
　　　　Now she holds her rooster
to her ear like a ticking package—rattle
　　　　in the breast of pooling
blood. She draws it out, lifting the head
　　　　of the bird into her mouth.

GATHERING THE MARE

Long after lightning ruined her
while she grazed at night
and we towed her roped up
behind the tractor to this slope
where clutches of buzzards
shuffled around her—pendants
of flesh swinging in their beaks—
where maggots, beetles, ants,
rain and sun cleaned and
bleached her—where rabbits
came to quarter and breed
beneath a bridge of bone
made by the arc of her ribs—
where hummingbirds thieved
away her forelocks to weave
and daub her into prim
white bowls, we climb back
to the clearing where she lies.
Green spill of briars from
the seams of her. My father
bending to coax them away
carefully—as though grooming
her—beads of blood scratch-
strung and welling at his wrists.
When she is free, he gets to
his knees to gather lost teeth
and the angled jawbone loosed
in a twist of weeds. He notes
that she still has the mouth
of a seven year old. Then,

pressing a boot to the absent
neck's curvature, he prises
her skull from the ground
and hands it to me. I hold it
out from my body like a bedpan.
In a feed sack he hides her
ribs away with what is left
of hoof and femur—undone
puzzle of vertebrae—and begins
to drag her toward a dense
front of honeysuckle and stunted
cedar—where we will leave her—
at the clearing's rim. He stops
and starts—his breath's work
small on the air. I follow, now
holding her skull to my chest.

SEASON

Albert Baker: 1921-1993

Dead on arrival at twenty-one—

        his memory not the crash

but freezing lost in the woods

        finding a trapper's cabin—

fire roars in the grate but

        no one's home—red fox pelt

by the hearth—

        soft, deflated length of the animal stretched

across stones—

        its lost eyes watching.

      •

Drought pasture and no hay—

        they deerpath the ridge at night—

the pinto, her coat gerrymandered

        into districts of milk and rust—

the yearling stallion soot-dark

        and raw in his architecture—

the mule (who we spot first)

        swishing, in a crush of the neighbor's

cabbages, his blonde tail—

        bucket of oats to shake them out, then

vault onto grainsacks to keep them at a trot

        as we drive—they pull

up to graze in a thin scar of clover

        down from the pasture's gate—

green strings of slobber blow forth

from the mule's lower lip—
they won't come further—
I'm ten—follow directions real good—
I run up and swing open the pasture gate—
plan is I'll turn them
when they come—
where's a switch to shoo them with—
but my father's already swatted
the stallion's hocks and barks
the clutch to juice the mare and mule
bucking into bolt—
muscular galloping panic—
the stallion thrashes his head to rip
the reins from the hands of an unseen rider—
I raise my arms
wide—barrier or martyr—
the stallion's mane rises away from
its crest—surge of dark strands—

·

Outside, a failing tobacco barn—
inside, twelve rows of wooden
bleachers around a clay pit
where men take bets on which bird
will kill the other first—
I'm five years old—it is freezing—cold
toes sting in their grubby boots—
men drink from steel flasks
near a pot-bellied stove
across the barn—my dad said to sit
right here and don't move—
I think that was a long time ago

•

Whoop and shush, whoop and shush.
He'd whipped the pregnant mare into
crossing low ground where three hills
shunted their runoff and she'd keeled
onto her side trapping his leg beneath her
in the bog. The whoop, which frightened
the mare, for someone to find him.
She'd then try to lift her head and right
herself, causing her rounded barrel
to torque against the trapped leg.
Therefore, the shush, which calmed
her head back down to the mud.

•

He rested his head on the pelt by the hearth
                    and felt an unreal warmth—
not on his skin but in his chest—
            then, the sense that once, long ago,
he'd wandered from the woods to this bare room.
                        He knew if he slept
he would not wake.

•

He bull-bellowed and bucked out
                of the barn and galloped in a tight
circle until there was a rough circumference
                        of blood in the dirt
which he fell into, rolling

onto his back in the center—hoofing
at the air like an equine beetle—
a red wash descending his backside
toward the tail—my father set
the testicles down on the rusted lid
of a feed barrel and we studied them.

•

The mule's mom was a smooth racking horse
and we'd ride him to show off the flawless gait
he'd inherited. The mule's dad was an ass.
After the mule balked in a roadside ditch—
trash-water up to his belly until my father beat
him out with a pole—we'd season him before
throwing on the saddle—all morning in plow-
harness, *haws* and *gees* turning him to break
the field—then hauling logs felled for pulp
from the woods—then the saddle—salt-lather
of sweat from his withers and steam wavering
from his despairing flanks. On their last ride,
when my father spurred the mule to the barn,
he broke into gallop and leapt up—hooves tight
and back arched—my father's face rose to strike
the entry's overhang and he flipped backwards
from the saddle to fall limp in mud and manure.

The mule trotted to hay without looking back.

·

During the depression
        the old folks couldn't wait to castrate something
so they could roll the balls in meal
                and fry them in a skillet popping
with lard and tear famished
                at the elastic knit of vesicles—*They'd call
them mountain oysters*, my father related.
                    Often, thereafter, I felt
on my person the weight of some eye watching—
                    eye of some forgotten
ancestor in a flour sack dress scrambling
                in a junk shack's clatterment
to scan through the warped boards
            as I passed—her wasp-nest tongue
searching over the toothless comb
            of her gums as her spectral eye—
eye that I could almost catch looking
            if I whipped around fast—
sized me up.

·

Rub of shut fists cold against his eyes—
                my father sits up
in the cabin—faint pulse wicks
            on the gurney in the hospital—
my uncle finds him—unsalvageable
            body shoved behind
a curtain until the doctor could correct
            the time-stamp

on death's paperwork—
                    he wipes the blackened face he cannot
recognize and guesses blood
                    from the smashed head is clotting
in my father's throat—past
                    the broken jaw a forced finger
looses what was blocking the breath—
                    what if the story cannot
escape the throat—
                    if no one comes to clear the passage?

                    •

All night we chase the dogs chasing game.
                    Youngest, I jog ahead
in the muscadine light—
                    keep them in earshot as they trail the game
ten times across a cold creek—
                    the game is smarter than we figure.
Near dawn, sting of sleet in sideways.
                    My father's flashlight spots
me locked up and shivering
                    in brambled thorns back up a muddy
draw.
    He untangles me and finds a place away from the wind
and pulls a mockingbird nest
                    from the dense cover of a cedar's
branches and puffs the dry twigs and meadow grass
                    to tinder
and strikes a fire in the hollow
                    of a rotting feeder log and grows
the heat with brittle limbs broken

       from a poplar that failed
to climb beyond the understory.
       Dogs come out of the dark—
the game is gone.
     They form a warm pack I sit in as sunrise
collapses white arches of ice
       lacing the briar-field shut.

     •

The army found fault with his feet—
      instead of Overlord, flat foot
to the floor of a Ford loaded with moonshine—
       dust boiling so thick
pursuit was impossible—
     even when they caught him, car crunched
against rock, the evidence in flames—
       that night, on a shelf
in a trapper's cabin, ink wicked
      behind the binding of this book.
When, in an ice storm after a botched hunt,
      he told me how he died,
my father mimicked my uncle
      mimicking the shock on a nurse's
face as she saw the dead man
      gasp and cough beside a metal pan
where dark blood had thickened
      into clots—my first words.

•

My father remembers a road
                        to the trestle—just there behind
the national park sign
                  where mountain kids have learned
to write their names:
                Triggerscratch & *Muzzlefont*—just there
in 1931, when he was my age now, and the trestle's steel
still rested on its concrete monoliths—
                     half mile up the creek
from its mouth just there—
                but this is 1982—summertime,
when a wobbling stream
              of RVs blights the park road until
their haul of pale bodies shine
                and writhe like larvae in every
good swimming hole—
            through the woods the creek back then
struck and parted around
              a beautiful flat-rock shoal where
he once spied as a boy just there
               a girl swim nude at dusk—
edge around a kudzu curtain and
               it is there—from fuller
woods distinct—above us a crease
               in the canopy not yet
healed over a vine-tangled alley of post oak and pines—

We'll have to go home and come back with the saws . . .

AT CHOTA:
FLOODED CHEROKEE CAPITOL

*"... some of the tribes have become extinct
and others have left but remnants to preserve
for awhile their once terrible names."*

—*Andrew Jackson to Congress, 1829*

The torched bush of the mind
Flickering out, thought
Flickering, becoming ash—
All night the lake read like a text
Written in watersnakes—
Bullfrogs, caught, sang
Death's language—foxfire,
Loosed breath of the drowned
Nation—whose ground we walk on—
What ground—whose laments we pray
Will not kindle—stripped bark
Of night—these waters pressing
Into—these red rocks
Quarried from the mountainside—
Seaside—Ordovician
Sediment broke upward
And America rose—glacial
Phosphate of dead sea animals—
Volcanic and eroding—
Utica mud shale—Trenton
Limestone—manifold cephalopods
And jawless fish-like vertebrates
Pressed in stone—preserved
Between the layers—locks

Of hair in a family Bible—
Confederates boxed in the stone—
Burial mounds troved
By the men of the state—
Tennessee Valley Authority—
Hydroelectric Lethe-waters—
Rank shimmer over the lost
Grounds—Sequoyah's syllabary's
Lost ash—Cherokee glottal
Ghost-music bubbling-up—
Surfacing snapping-turtles—
Vicious, lethargic, prehistoric—
Mind out—it seemed each sunrise
Pressed its dire eye to a keyhole,
Beyond which memory—Mother—
Rose from her youthful bath,
Loosening her terrible jaw—

POLYPHONIC

Cicadas chorusing at the treeline—
swarm of engines that will not fire—
and I remember half-acre sheets
of tobacco gauze we'd unroll
over seedlings—odd synesthesia
of insect chirr and a childhood
memory of staking these blank
banners in spring chill. What binds
the buzz to the gauze so that each
rev starts inside me (what exactly)?
Rectangles of sonic? Shrill bolts?

•

It is the males who sing, rattling
abdominal timbals to call their mates.
When a mess of them get going
there is a certain undulation—
the gauze, too, undulated. Back then
I'd press the side of my face to the dirt
to see gold-green seedlings beneath
their makeshift greenhouse—sticky
waft of tobacco and turned earth—
scent-sting of fertilizer and manure
on wavelengths of air lifting the sheer
cloth. Unlike the cicada, we don't slip
our husks and still sing. The carapace
turns white with rosin, forelegs hooked
into the bark of a pine. One morning
my father fell and a fog came whispering

over his face. Any word that might have
lifted him had already climbed black
rungs of smoke where the winter grass
was burned away. Root-systems in
the red clay clods the tractor turned—
the white fingers of denotation dying.

•

Thick gray loom of Appalachian sky.
*Diaphanous cacophony? Threadbare
clamor?* The Cherokee tell of
a hummingbird who breathed smoke
into the nostrils to revive the dead.
Once I sparked flint in the dark
and in that flicker a damp field
covered with blank sheets. No spark
landed. No shoots of smoke rose
as the mite-sized tobacco seeds
of flame fell from my hands. Steel
knocking to stone the only sound—
my father appeared at the treeline
holding out an empty bridle.

•

The goddess, Eos, begged Zeus
to make immortal her human lover,
Tithonus, who thereafter merely
withered with age until he shrank
into the form of a cicada and whirred
eternal. I click my tongue and tremor
my larynx to say TREE: yellow

caterpillars tented in a black cherry
next to the field ready to be planted.

•

Incessant bandages? Dissonant shrouds?
Language is, of course, gibberish
all the way up to the ear, but beyond
the ear there are pathways of fire—
a here—where this grove of rattling
bugs is saying *Love me! Kill me!*
Are you there? Beyond the ear, these
blank panels are making their own
racket. They are not scattered
eardrums in the field, but the seedlings
beneath, like fine cochlear hairs,
are capturing all the perturbations
of our coming and going to feed them
back to the earth from which we came.

•

Because the pathways lead me back
to here (where we both stood when you
still lived), because we pulled this fabric
taut in our four hands and staked it,
because this is what we unrolled, this
flag of the country of your final
surrender—this is your voice
(which can carry) spread out
and fastened to the ground to trouble
the air in a language that fills in all
the blanks between us. Language

wafting molecules to the nostrils —
language riding light to the back
of the eye. Now a whippoorwill starts
up an ether of apple-rot. Now a bullfrog
croaks vertigo (wobbling on the boat's
bow). Now a red fox lopes the blood-
iron-flesh of fresh liver from the treeline.
Now a cricket heats the scar where you
tore my ankle with the barb of a gig.

•

When the cicadas stop singing,
the mountaintop will already be crimson-
gold and the immense falling, scattering
and gathering of autumn will come
peeling slowly down the fissured slopes
until we are forced in by the wind.
We know that buds, in time, will climb
up bursting — winching up slightly
each day until they reach the ridge.
How nice to think this unrolling
blossoming does not stop there,
but climbs beyond the peak into the air
toward a precipice we cannot see.
As long as the cicadas are singing, let us
stay here — jar flies you would call them.
You tied the end of a thread to the leg
of one caught, and the other end
to my forefinger. We ran in the field
tethered that way — me on the ground
and the insect flying above.

BLUE YODEL

T for Texas, T for Tennessee—
                    some kid (maybe eighteen) busking
the corner of Beale and Main—
                    his case with its lining of black felt
open for us to fill—
                    T for Thelma, that gal made a wreck out of me.
It's almost comic, this wisp
                    of a boy pushing pale into tradition's
turbid waters with his weathered Martin—
                    six silk and steel strings—
to prop himself up.
                    What would he know about Jimmie Rodgers?
Jimmie a runaway by thirteen—
                    smear of burnt cork covering
his face—playing minstrel
                    in medicine shows until his railman
father found him and drug him back.
                    Jimmie dead by thirty-five,
wasted body on blood-specked sheets
                    at the Taft Hotel—in his last
recording, unaccompanied
                    two days before, his father's warning
still haunting the lyrics,
                    You'll be sorry that you're roaming.

•

Our busker thumps brusquely
                    through Jimmie's old boasts—
I'm a Tennessee Hustler and I don't have to work.
                                        He threatens
I'm gonna buy me a pistol just as long as I am tall
and looses the yodel's whirling
                        hyperbole—a curling claim
that he knows what it is to run from loneliness
                            only to get hauled
back, what it is to get nailed up
                    on those three crucifix Ts: Texas,
Tennessee, and Thelma.
                        To be true, if Jimmie was the root of
anything, it was someone else's water
                        he pulled up—the poetry
of men he worked and played with
                        rail to rail—their blue songs
rolling tongue to tongue to tongue
                        until their pranks and pains
were loosed from ten thousand throats.

•

Now, I would like to say a few words

                                         about existential semiotics,

the broad-faced man had warned

                                        through the dark pinwheel

of his goatee that morning as I wandered

                                        daftly into the wrong

lecture.

    Sheepish, I stayed and learned of lost states of being—
ideas unknown, emotions

                                unfeelable—I grasped at silhouettes

of those things that cannot be

                                uttered, cannot be graphed

or sung because no words, no notes,

                                no signs have ever grafted

onto them.

          Afterwards, I drifted immaterial from the vast and
mooringless hall—

          I was the air where once, long ago, a glyph
of smoke rose.

•

The kid's guitar has a crack in the bridge.

A tattoo's trapped ink
dips beneath his shirt sleeve—

dark lines, unrecognizable without
context, resembling a worm perched on a hook.

Is he aware
that we are rung with this

infinity of the inaccessible—unheard
melodies no hands can ever play?

How, otherwise, could he swell
up like a rooster and crow

these horrors Thelma has wrought—
betrayals surely no crossties of

language, no other warbling station
of notes, could name?

I drop his felt a dollar—a green glossolalia
for our time—and his nod

acknowledges me in rhythm with
his foot.

Then the song starts waving its *Special* to frighten off
the *rounders*.

·

Later I look up busker

          to trace the word's roots back to water.
English ships, when tacking around

          bad weather, were described
as *busking it out*. In Old Spanish boscar

          meant to hunt by making
a noise of the woods to scare

          out game. In Old French busquer
meant *to filch, prowl, catch by hook or crook*

          and—in the vulgate,
buscare: *to shift for*.

          What must be crossed—language, thought
and flesh—the three Ts—

          to find the Protean water no hand can
cup—I think of the roots, of the three

          auditory ossicles in
the mammal ear, and how two strayed

          from the articulating
jaws of reptilian precursors . . .

•

There is no new —

        there is only the ancient we have yet to name —
estranged ancient that we call out to

                with worn song —
peals of gospel, star paths

           of Navajo chant, floats of mantra,
the minaret loosing

         prayer, flamenco's spry caterwauls, banjo
pickers' whiskey

        hollers, the boy of thirteen learning to shape
the blessing, the freedman

           yodeling over the herd at night,
Are you there?

        to the Swiss cowboy who taught him Alp-speak —
roots — our *via tuberosa* —

           pulling the unchartable water
up and across the transom

         of tiny bones in the inner ear
so that we quaver with its

           arrival and others can see,
within us, sign.

When you see roots, call out—

                           Teyshas, the Caddo word

for *friends*—Tanasi, Cherokee

                               for where the water bends—

Thelma, Greek for volition.

                        I hold my hand before my mouth

and say *death*—as in the moment

                              of my expiration—

I feel a warm expulsion of breath.

                           If I say *dead*—as in

what comes after breathing—

                         no air strikes my hand.

Word grafted, word in the flesh.

Soon enough the sun
　　　　　　sunk to haul us back to its blind shed.
Soon enough Thelma
　　　　　　come to the joint, a .44 in each hand.
Take this brakeman's lantern—
　　　　　　it's used for signaling—
we're going to creep through
　　　　　　the deep woods to shift
and pilfer and prowl.
　　　　　　Tuck that Special under your belt—
we're going to open the case
　　　　　　where the wide river
only knows us when we howl.

GAUNT SERENADE

Sunset a swollen throat—and nothing so effusive as
        this little city infinite with combustion,
where civilization piles up at intersections—its engines
        exact waves of fire around camshafts
spinning—tornadoes of teeth that gnaw the last morsels
        of quietude from the bone; silence is
nothing to mourn—even the humdrum rhythmias of
        the animal heart will turn perfectly
still air into a bear trap of shockwave concentric around
        the body, even a forest has its bird-knock
and wind-sputter—why *not* live here: where planes
        pay out worms of vapor to the sky, or
descending, dissect the ether with a scalpel of reflected
        light, where concrete trucks inseminate
suburban basements with flumes of hardening slop—
        where want is appeasable *24 Hours*
at a fluorescent Vatican of weeping produce, where men
        burst through double doors wheeling
their bucket and their mop—where the flayed fist
        of a factory tomato punches along an aorta
of metal tubing to arrive at the dumbfounded solace
        of its can—where the lurching symphonic
of train intersects with the scat-sluice gurgling of river—
        where last shafts of light glow like bolts
in the x-ray of a fractured hip—and night closes
        its garage door over the hospital,
bringing its extreme unction and *coup de grâce?*

THE RECESSION

There is a statue of Saint George in the park
     we might bed or bury under
and there the bronze genitalia of his steed
     would make strange moons,
offering the only ingotfuls of light this city
     might offer; and there rested
we might wander again among the hard cases—
     toss our last dimes to hats
that line the street like black holes at pickers'
     tapping feet, our final bright
coins pulled away like accelerating stars until
     somebody'd say *You guys*
are angels, you know that! and we'd stop
     to give over to him our bottle
and our smokes and note the sound hole
     of his guitar—how it'd seem
to bow in about the bridge and fret board
     toward that density of dark
and we'd know that when next he tuned
     flat to sharp the sound hole
would collapse both instrument and him;
     but we'd push on sobering
the worn gold of testicle-light past grain lofts—
     gargantuan and sadly epic
beside the broken-windowed brewery—past
     the once sumptuous façade
of the condemned theater, crumbling marquis
     above ornamental columns,
dead air-conditioners thrusting huge rumps
     into the street, flanked

on either side by age-sooted alabaster divas—
    and we'd swing on out
into night on nothing but one slender tendril
    of defeat to name all the faces
streaming like gargoyles between the stoops
    of the buildings boarded up
and slated for catastrophe; later, we'd likely
    inhabit a stool at the all-night
spoon on Olive Street, savoring the hypnotic
    power of grease, iridescent
and swirling in our cups of double-black . . .
    There the kitchen floor always
an ice-rink of lard and the night cook always
    barefoot, streaming sweat
and blinking in the grill's steam as he scrubs
    it all down. Here is the slow
burn-off, the sulfurous incense which even
    the waitress camped beside
the disconnected pay-phone winces at, which
    explains everything about
this city. Here always a note of blood hanging
    in the air. Here no one ever
looks us in the eye and any with an elsewhere
    soon begins to sense a jangling
unease like a chestful of keys. When one duo
    here parting manages *I love you*
it bruises us deep like a shotgun kicking back
    into the shoulder. Here
it's going to be a long, long time before anyone
    gets anything they can eat.

SOMNILOQUY AGAINST SPRING

Please, not so soon.
For now let me be simplified —
          no face, just a dull
push of electricity descending
          the spine. What if
I wake tomorrow to geese
          formationed
for descent, or waddling out
          onto broken ice —
or to robins, with breasts like
          something gnawed
open, pestering the ground
          for worms? How
could the plates of my skull
          hold together
if the fractalizations of ice
          melted and broke
and rode back into the trees?
          If the chemical green
fire lit up again in the grass?
          If the velocity
of misspelling accelerated
          in the suturing
of genes? Since I am welded
          so tightly to zero,
tomorrow no cardinals like
          ingots of blood
in the branches, no molecules
          of piss unlocking
their stink in the alleyways, no

dogwoods thrusting
cups of nail holes in my face,
no one waving
a gun on a day so beautiful
you had forgotten
the knife at the throat
of simplest
comprehension. Before that,
leave me this
featureless sleep a while longer.
Let me be made
stupider than humanly possible,
or let me wake
to more winter, where offcast
bottles tumor
a bare and birdless thicket.

OBESE AUBADE

Long rain, the air unwieldy
with worm-must, spring mush, apple-
simmerings, a fishlip of
moon waxing to black, one star
raveling its wick-light down
to the flood-line, varicose
gutters' currents of offal—
crushed butts, sand-salt, leaf decay—
dawn gouging at the tree line,
robins like blood-stars scared up,
the branches finned, manifold
gold-green leaf-shoots—visible,
becoming, and dawn-steady
the light pushing, light pushing
through the tree line like a riot
squad, light quarantining from
shadow the scrub-brush thickets,
air becoming wavery
with evaporate, rising
water-fume over the turned
soil and wheat-shear, over
winter's broken ice-sutures,
and day now a conception
pressing outward flesh-colored
dawn, lowering the stomach
of it somewhere to the west,
day now with its styluses
ratcheting up over grooved
twig-and-straw nests, orange-lined
warbler-mouths prised open—

carnivorous flowers—young
feathered in wet dandelion-
shag, sleep-bobbing—sudden throat—
musculature corseting
down on its song, then marsh frogs
pick-up blustering at chest-
throat sails, grackles serrating
the airwaves, nearby suburbs
revving for commute—emptying
away from this landscape, its
flesh and feather fattening
out with sound, its screech-caw-lilts,
thin peep-peeps strained from needle-
sized wind tunnels, meat-fetter
bird tongues fire-flickering in
tooth-sized beaks—yellow-breasted,
ruby-rumped, crimson-throated . . .

GRAZING

You are right in between a beautiful graveyard
                    and a beautiful river,
but not terribly far from the slaughterhouse
                    whose entire syllabary
consists of one long vowel.
                    Here is a place where you can watch
the sky—thin clouds left over to the west
                    like bits of gristle—
and the river is golden,
                    a strip of police tape this time of day.
Your server, it seems, has cut his hand
                    though you had only asked
for water—he weeps so bravely in his gauze.
                    The presence of blood
is not undesirable in the presentation,
                    yet the key criteria remain
texture, coloration, juiciness, and marbling.
                    The pneumatic bolt
is the preferred mode of execution—
                    though hair, skull fragments,
and tissue may be sent convolving inward—
                    making it improbable
that the brain will pass inspection.
                    Sunlight strikes the dormitories.
In the primest of cuts fat is an *interlacing*.
                    They've all left you here
without your bill and no one
                    has brought a straw so you, wrongly
toothed, might avoid the pain of sipping.
                    Remember the airplane?

How cows and farm houses—odd implements—
                         cast long shadows
on the prairie.
        Grain silos a mile long in evening light—so they've
left you here without your bill.
                        There are rules, patterns. Are we
not bound?
        Now the contrails redden like incisions in the west.
Day is performing its own autopsy
                         in the most delightful way.
There is a silhouette in the opening-up
                         that is in shape and contour
heartlike.
    There, a darkening weight falls out like a liver. It is only
in the cleanest kills the mind is left intact.
                         At the graveyard they have
a list of everyone who will not have to die.
                         They keep it there on little,
separate stones.
        Sixteen pig iron pike points guard the asphalt drive.
Dormitory is where you sleep.
                         Will someone be coming soon?
The slaughterhouse has filled with hush
                         and now it is raining so
very lightly as if the sky were trying
                         to send the earth a message
without your knowing.
                 When you look closely, at certain angles,
you can see the immensity of the conversation
                         and there they are
on the cobblestones—
                 entire languages written in evaporating ink.

RESOLUTION

Whereas in the afterlife Verb will be a mute;
Whereas, knowing such, Verb is nouning noon and night;
Whereas the Milky Way, with its distant froth of stars,
       resembles the mongrel snout of something rabid;
Whereas the full moon is the terrified eye of the black
       mare;
Whereas even the dimmest street may lead to the cold sea;
Whereas the foghorns blare *More fog! More fog!* into this
       fog;
Whereas the horizon lops off the head of the sun;
Whereas day soon drops a jailhouse through the clouds;
Whereas the wind seems absurdly susurrus in those
       swaying trees that circle the planetarium;
Whereas it is nearly time for Time to stand in its flooded
       basement;
Whereas someone yells *Action!* and Action does laps in
       its cell;
Whereas men are climbing out of the sewers—climbing
       back in;
Whereas Verb must do that;
Whereas Verb must weigh each syllable as he hops on the
       freight yard scales;
Whereas no one can say which whether is accurate or
       whether what is trued;
Whereas, despite such, Verb must make audible a line of
       his mother's face;
Whereas, despite such, Verb must have the poem shuffle
       its feet like his father in the aisles of a liquor store;
Whereas Verb knows it would be easier for a cobweb to
       capture a tree;

Whereas Verb knows it would be easier for the hospital's
blind janitor to squint through his larynx;
Whereas this must all be done before the black lid is
pulled down over the bald eye of the dead mare—
the new moon;
Whereas the stars are far too large for the snare pole with
its little loop of rope—nor will they be goaded into
the cage of vapors on the back of Verb's plain
white truck;
Whereas the doctor, long deceased, once wrote: *Ars longa,
vita brevis*;
Therefore, when the pen breaks, Verb is resolved to note
how his black fingernails resemble the shut wings
of a roach.

UPON LOOKING INTO A HIGH
SCHOOL PHOTOGRAPHY EXHIBIT
AT A STRIP MALL

Here a horse stock-still, sectioned behind planks
       in his enclosure. Here kittens
in unroustable slumber arrayed. Here sunlight
       too golden on a slate of water,
too frisky in greeting each curdled cloud. Here
       summits enveil their haunts
with mists. Here snowflake. Here feather. Here
       elderly hands afloat in sepia
glooms. And here, one sophomore named Trish
       has hung a muddled time-lapse
of an umbrella magnolia blossoming—a work
       she has entitled *Self-portrait*.
After a long look, I do have a sense of a blurred
       sway of petals loosed by light
and I'm thinking I can track a first curious car
       meandering on the freeway
of the bee, can see dew's crystal reflective scoops
       apparitioning to vapor . . .
Aren't we all walking chronologies who cannot
       keep our place? Aren't we
each, like Trish, too much was and will-be
       collapsed in a single frame?
An octogenarian's adolescent face can be seen
       within a prankish glance,
and the too-young bride on her wedding day
       may well appear at the funeral
in the widow's sudden blush. To take things
       further, consider: each particle

of light is from a separate age—photons born
        hundreds, thousands, millions
of years apart during fusion in the sun's dense
        core, all escaped its gravity
at once eight minutes past to just now together
        pierce this strip mall glass
and illuminate *Self-portrait*. Then consider stars,
        each a sun heralding a time
long past. Which have dimmed or died? We're all
        like you Trish—hazy portraits
hung in now's polytemporal light, simultaneities—
        as if the octogenarian's mother
cries out in labor just as his daughter is leaning
        over the coffin to kiss his
folded hands—as if the constellate age spots
        on his dead wrists are being
loaded onto the helixes that made him. Now all
        the widow's incarnations
turn light back to every eye that ever glimpsed
        her as her hand is grasping
the rounded doorknob—her excarnation waiting
        one turn away. Or, flung
open now, the strict modality of the hearse as we
        together look gawkish past
the windshield's wipers at a spectrum of visible
        us. We whose genome holds
the history of a species and all our possibilities.
        We who were once fire-flung
stumps of carbon cooked in a dying sun. We
        finites neverending. We troves
of happening. We hives innumerable humming
        with familiar ghosts. We holds.

We echoes. We harmonies. Everlasting We
adrift in the lacteal wash of stars.

ACKNOWLEDGMENTS

Appreciation to the following publications in which earlier versions of some of these poems have appeared:

American Letters and Commentary: "Louis vs. Louis"
Best New Poets 2010: "April Blizzard"
Blackbird: "Season," and "Three Fluid Graces"
Boxcar Poetry Review: "Ouroborus"
Copper Nickel: "At Chota: Flooded Cherokee Capitol" and "Caliban at Bikini"
Cream City Review: "Grazing"
The Cortland Review: "Graceland"
Cutbank: "Story"
Day One: "Upon Looking into a High School Photography Exhibit at a Strip Mall"
The Distillery: "Gathering the Mare"
Phoebe: "Obese Aubade" and "Somniloquy against Spring"
The South Dakota Review: "Gaunt Serenade"
The Southern Poetry Review: "The Mechanic's Daughter"
Town Creek Poetry: "Polyphonic"
Washington Square: "Jacksonville"

"At Chota: Flooded Cherokee Capitol" was selected for inclusion in *The Southern Poetry Anthology Vol. VI: Tennessee,* Edited by Jesse Graves, Paul Ruffin, and William Wright, Texas Review Press, 2013.

"Upon Looking into a High School Photography Exhibit at a Strip Mall" was selected for inclusion in *Day One, Year One: Best New Stories and Poems, 2014,* edited by Carmen Johnson.

An excerpt from the poem "Story" appeared in *The Philadelphia Inquirer.*

This work owes a debt to many, but especially to the insight and brilliance of these friends and mentors: Kevin Christianson, James Galvin, Bryan Hunter, Allison Inman, Nancy Mendoza and Nick Regiacorte. I am also grateful for the generous feedback of Dorianne Laux and Joseph Millar, and for the incredible work of Christine Holbert.